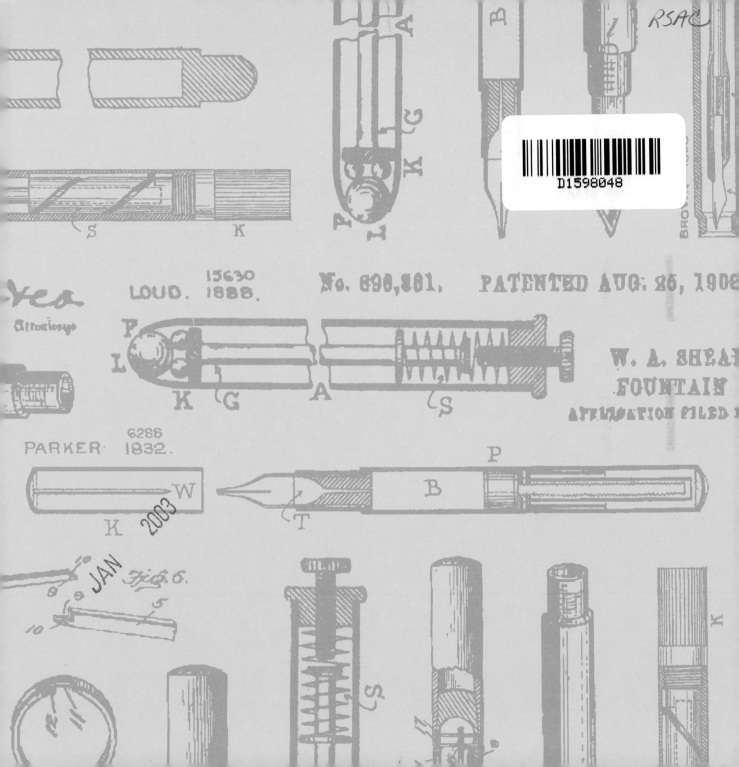

FOUNTAIN PENS

JONATHAN STEINBERG

FOUNTAIN PENS

THEIR HISTORY AND ART

UNIVERSE

First published in the United States of America in 2002 by

UNIVERSE PUBLISHING

A Division of Rizzoli International Publications, Inc.

300 Park Avenue South

New York, NY 10010

Copyright © 2001 by Jonathan Steinberg

All rights reserved. No part of this publication may be reproduced, stored in a retrieval system, or transmitted in any form or by any means, electronic, mechanical, photo-copying, recording, or otherwise, without prior consent of the publisher.

2002 2003 2004 2005 2006 / 10 9 8 7 6 5 4 3 2 1

Printed in China

Library of Congress Control Number: 2002103457

Design by Paul Kepple and Timothy Crawford at Headcase Design.

Photographs © Paul Forrester and Maurizio Minelli

page 5: Parker eye dropper from around 1910 known to collectors as the ribbon design. This pen has been found in a very small number of examples and although there is one in the Parker archive in Janesville, which confirms that it was not an unauthorized jeweller-made design, it was never mentioned in the company's adver-tising. It seems to have been a hand made special order as the design of each pen is slightly different.

681.6 S819f 2002
Steinberg, Jonathan.
Fountain pens : their histor
and art

*To my wife, Nancie, who stood for a lot
while I was writing the accompanying
work and my mother who accidentally
involved me in all this.*

TABLE OF CONTENTS

INTRODUCTION

RECENTLY THE FOUNTAIN PEN HAS COME BACK INTO WIDESPREAD GENERAL USE AND WITH IT, interest in vintage pens has proliferated. "Flagship" limited editions, usually designed in the vintage style, are often marketed to give allure to the manufacturer's main pen lines, making it difficult to determine which is the chicken and which is the egg in this trend: It is unclear whether people have suddenly become interested in pens as such or, rather, if interest has been revived because of these advertising blitzes for new pens in the vintage style.

Until the early 1980s, pen design hadn't moved forward significantly in decades. It seemed that the pen companies were content to let ballpoint pen sales drive their profits. There was a general belief that the fountain pen market was stagnant and that nothing could be done to revive it. Old designs had been largely forgotten, and modern designs were for the

most part lackluster. Indeed, one company was still selling its higher end pens using cosmetics unchanged since the 1940s.

From the mid-1970s to the mid-1980s, three separate factors emerged that changed the complexion of the vintage pen market. First, in about 1976, Christie's in London started holding sales of vintage pens; collectors who met at those sales were galvanized to start the Writing Equipment Society. Second, in the early 1980s, a group of collectors in Chicago began holding meetings to discuss and trade vintage pens; these meetings

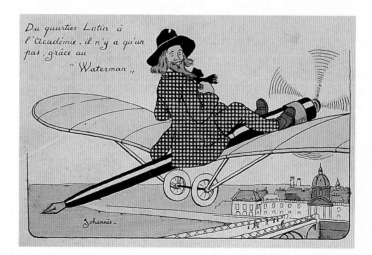

gradually evolved into formal pen shows around the United States. And third, a few books on fountain pens were published; initially these publications were distributed to American collectors in small numbers, but soon they were made available to the public. The most widely distributed of these was an Italian book, *La Penna,* by Emilio Castruccio. At last the public began to notice that fountain pens were more than just that cheap piece of plastic they had used at school, and the pen collecting movement gained momentum.

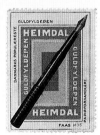

Unlike the market for other collectables, such as wrist watches, the pen market is not uniform around the world. Patek Philippes and Rolexes are the most desirable commercial watches worldwide, and their value at auction is uniform whether in London, Los Angeles, or Hong Kong. The fountain pen market is much more regionalized. American collectors collect solely American pens and favor the 1880s–1910s "eyedroppers." German and Italian collectors prefer German and Italian pens respectively, but when they do buy American pens, such as Parker Duofolds (and in the case of Italian collectors, Sheaffers), the value of those pens are entirely different from that in the United States. And there are still huge markets where pen collecting just hasn't yet taken off. This may account for long periods of relative stability in prices.

Curiously, this contemporary taste for collecting fountain pens reflects the initial level of public interest that companies experienced with those same pen designs when they were new. In certain countries, the public just wasn't ready to

[1]
Montblanc No. 124E + 73E piston filler sets, including the rare "Roses" pattern, 1930s.

[1]
**Montblanc Moore-type safety and
straight lever filler**
[2]
**The original Safety Pen Patent in
patent form.**
[3]
**The original Sheaffer lever filler
in patent form.**

[1]

accept radically different designs or technological advances in
writing instruments.

In Germany, for example, Montblanc (then called the
Simplo Filler Pen Company, selling pens under the name
Rouge et Noir) was a company very much in tune with its market. They initially sold eyedroppers for a short period before
they standardized production around the safety pen, which

[2]

remained in production in various guises until the late 1930s.
At that time the safety was generally considered by pen companies worldwide to be a very old-fashioned design, but companies like Montblanc knew what their market wanted—so much so
that later Montblanc safeties (the 102-108 series) were even
designed to look like more up-to-date self-filling models.
Although as the 1920s wore on Montblanc did make self-filling
pens such as the rare lever fillers based on the Sheaffer design,

W. A. SHEAFFER.
FOUNTAIN PEN.
APPLICATION FILED MAR. 2, 1908.

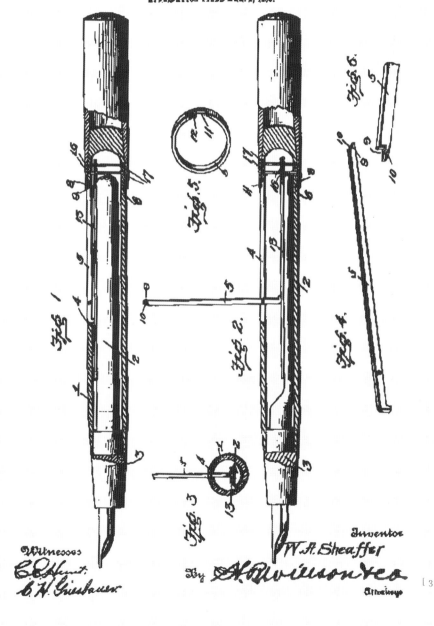

Witnesses
C. C. Hunt.
C. W. Giesbauer.

Inventor
W. A. Sheaffer
By Wilson & Co
Attorneys

[3]

and the even rarer blow fillers (a mechanism copied from Crocker and Chilton), the company was convinced that their home market wanted the tried and true older technology, so the Montblanc pens made with these newer and more sophisticated technologies were exported.

The current renaissance of interest in vintage pens has been spurred, at least in part, by users realizing that the vintage pens write completely differently from modern pens. Although new pens are better designed than those produced between the 1940s and 1960s, they simply do not write as well as the older ones. The reason is the difference between a flexible and a rigid nib. For about a thousand years, writing had been accomplished with quills, all of which had points that

„My grandmother's ear trumpet has been struck by lightning" *ballpoint*

„My grandmother's ear trumpet has been struck by lightning" *Esterbrook 14*

„My grandmother's ear trumpet has been struck by lightning" *Waterman 1908's 2*

[2]

[1]

were very flexible. The earliest fountain pens emulated the flexibility of quills. Rigid nibs were produced but were regarded as an oddity; they were used mostly for writing through numerous copies of carbon paper. For this reason they were called "manifold" nibs.

Soon after the introduction of lifetime warranties in the 1920s, however, companies could no longer offer flexible nibs because flexible nibs tended to bend or break more often than rigid ones. Companies forced to produce rigid nibs marketed them by emphasizing the nib's smoothness to draw attention away from its rigidity. Even worse, during the late 1930s and 1940s, the effects of the Depression and wartime exigencies mandated the use of much smaller amounts of gold, in nibs, making

[1]
Montblanc, 1910s. In the 1910s and 1920s, Montblanc experimented with a number of lever-filling mechanisms. This exceptionally rare lever-filler is known to collectors in only one example worldwide.
[2]
Handwriting sample showing variation between ballpoint (top), fountain pen (middle), and vintage fountain pen (bottom).
[3]
Rare red mottled 1920s Rouge et Noir button filler No. 4 pen.

[3]

[1]

Two celluloid lever filling pens made by Wahl-Eversharp in the 1930s. Above, a brown and gold Doric dating from 1935. Below, a jade green 1932 Deco Band. Both of these pens have a nib which was adjustable from flexible to rigid by moving the slider along its length. This was a more successful method of varying the nib style used by Wahl-Eversharp after they had initially tried an interchangeable "Personal Point" nib/feed unit.

them harder than ever. In response, companies emphasized how quickly the ink dried.

Thus, not only had mass production rendered pens themselves less attractive by the 1950s and 1960s, the beautiful, individualized handwriting produced by flexible nibs had disappeared as the public had accepted rigid nibs decades earlier. The stage was set for future generations to rediscover how beautiful fountain pens had been and how beautifully they wrote.

Various books on fountain pens have been written but most have followed similar formats, looking at pens either by country or by manufacturer. Unfortunately, most companies, and

[1]

all countries, tend to look the same when featured in this manner: Most started producing pens in the last part of the nineteenth century or the first few decades of the twentieth. Most produced eyedroppers until they went over to lever fillers. Most foundered during the Depression, and most companies went so far down-market thereafter that they went broke after the largely coincidental introduction of the ballpoint.

In this book I present what I feel was significant in the development of the fountain pen and the fountain pen market during the twentieth century. This format will assist the reader in understanding why fountain pen technology or pen companies' models developed in the way they did. Any particular companies not discussed were not, in my view, significant in the development or marketing of the fountain pen. This judgment, of course, has no bearing whatsoever on whether the pens were of high quality or whether the reader may consider them collectable.

[2]
Rouge et Noir, 1915.

[2]

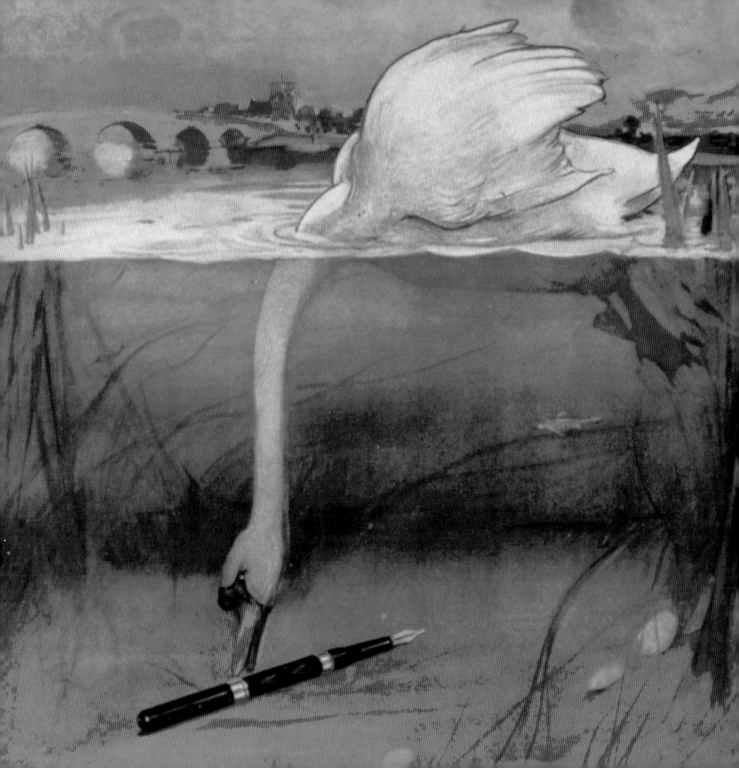

CHAPTER ONE

PRE-1880S: BEFORE THE FOUNTAIN PEN

The commercial development of the fountain pen reflected the development of industrial society. Its invention occurred at a late stage in the industrial revolution, most likely because up until that time, most people did not do much writing. Most large-scale writing projects could be accommodated by either the printing press or rooms full of inexpensive scribes equipped with quills. Moreover, it was hardly up to those scribes being offered work (or the opportunity to learn how to write) to criticize the writing instrument. It was just accepted that the only tool available was a quill. That it needed dipping in ink every few words was considered unimportant.

By the end of the eighteenth century, things started to change. It became common for people in positions of authority to want to write—sometimes quite a lot. Those peo-

[1]

French shagreen case holding silver inkwell with holder, nib, and porte crayon; c. 1765.

[2]

English tortoiseshell case with two inkwells, seal, universal holder for knifeblade and three different guage silver nibs; c. 1780.

[1]

ple often had access to artisans who could create whatever they needed, including a more efficient writing instrument. And such people may well on occasion have liked tinkering with technology.

Thus was born the desire for a working fountain pen that would contain a reservoir of ink that would automatically feed the point. But producing one wasn't easy. The problem is that when ink flows down the nib to the paper it tends to create a vacuum inside the barrel. After the initial flow of whatever ink lays on the nib or quill, no further ink will flow. Attempts to force more ink from the reservoir to the nib often resulted in blobs of ink finding their way onto the paper.

Ultimately, of course, it was recognized that a channeled "feed" meters the amount of ink getting to the paper because air passes up the channel into the reservoir in the opposite direction of the ink.

Thomas Jefferson was one inventor obsessed with how to meter the flow of ink to the nib properly. His work as an international statesman and landowner led to prolific per-

[2]

[1]

[2]

[3]

[1]
French 18-carat gold dip pen in
form of a feather, ca. 1840.
[2]
English silver gilt Penmanship
Prize with integral nib, 1831.
[3]
English silver pen in the form of
a feather by John Jago, ca. 1820.

[4]

A group of Southern and Northern Asian styluses constructed of iron, some with silver decoration, ca. A.D. 800.

[1]
French gold double-ended twist-
action pen with gold tubular nib
and gold pencil, ca. 1830, decorated in blue enamel with white
enamel lettering: "Gage sincere et
durable de bonne amitie."
[2]
Italian all-steel double-ended
slide action spear nib with porte
crayon, ca. 1780.
[3]
French ivory gold-studded pen
with gold tubular nib and porte
crayon, ca. 1780.
[4]
English bone traveling pen with
gilt tubular nib, ca. 1800.
[5]
French ivory pen with gold tubular
nib, mounts, and porte crayon,
ca. 1770.

sonal writing, which was hampered by the frequent dipping required by quill pens. As a highly educated man, Jefferson liked occupying himself with technology, so it was almost inevitable that sooner or later he would turn his attentions to simplifying the task of writing.

Jefferson found his solution in the topography of his estate at Monticello. It was situated at the crest of a small hill, beneath which ran a stream. Elaborate devices were designed to make it easier to bring the water from the stream up to the house. Jefferson adapted this technology for the fountain pen, trying to put a "buffer" ink supply within the writing instrument. It worked as follows: Establish a supply of ink—a large bottle similar to the stream. Feed the ink to the nib and have it collect at the back of the nib as a small, second reservoir. From this reservoir, the quill can draw through a slit to feed ink to the paper. So the pen will write for more than just a few words, until the small reservoir is exhausted, and the whole hand doesn't have to be taken away from the paper to dip every few seconds.

[1]

[2]

[3]

[4]

[5]

[1]
Diagram of a Bion.
[2]
**Early example of the Bion principle
reservoir pen, ca. 1725.
Constructed in brass with shagreen around the barrel, this pen
uses a quill cut nib secured
around a tubular "feed." The feed
acts as the receptor for the screw
plug mounted inside the cap. It
unscrews at the seal end, and the
seal is a nobleman's profile. The
pen would be filled and then
plugged with wood cork before the
seal end was reattached.**

Although clearly an advance over the dipping pen, this implement couldn't have worked particularly well as it lacked a channeled feed to meter that ink flow to that second, "buffer" reservoir. Indeed, in 1824, Jefferson wrote to a friend that he had come across a fountain pen patented by Cowan. He noted that Cowan's pen worked better than any

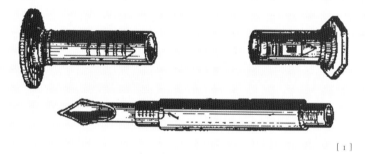

[1]

fountain pens he had ever seen, especially the Bion, which was then the standard method of inserting a reservoir into the barrel of a pen.

But this was an age in which information was not disseminated widely. There was no wide-scale patenting of inventions and no mass publication of articles about how to

make writing easier. Those who weren't inventors or tinker-
ers would approach a craftsman (usually a silversmith) and
tell him what kind of pen was wanted. He would ask around
and then design something using the latest innovations for
obviating the need to keep dipping the quill into the ink.
Some craftsmen near the end of the eighteenth century used
something like Hodgson's Patent, also known as the Sheffer
Pen-O-Graphic. This carried the ink inside the barrel in a
pig's bladder held apart with balsa-wood slats. On the side of
the barrel was a button that was supposed to fit closely with
the positioning of the hand when writing. Without taking the
hand away from the writing position the button could be
depressed and a large blob of ink fed onto the quill. The
quill was cut at the writing end, so ink would feed through
the cut to the writing point of the quill. Initially, a lever was
included on the side that would have been pulled back when
the button was depressed in order to admit ink to the feed
area, but soon it was found that ink could be metered in a
rudimentary fashion without this lever.

[2]

[1]

John Jacob Parker's 1832 patent

[2]

Bion pen constructed of high-carat gold and mother-of-pearl, ca. 1765. The end, with decreasing scale marks, is the cap to the pen, which, like the pen at left, uses a gold hollow nib secured around a tubular "feed" that acts as the receptor for the screw plug. The other end, with the shorter cap, houses a simple ring-clamp porte crayon in gold with a leather disk that doubles as a plug to the ink reservoir.

Although Hodgson's Patent was fairly well known among some craftsmen, there were no large-scale production processes in place to make this invention commercially available and no publicity for such limited-interest inventions. Thus, different craftsmen attempting to make a continuous-flow writing instrument approached the problem in different ways. During the 1830s, an English craftsman-inventor named John Jacob Parker

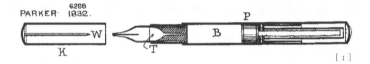

[1]

devised another solution to the problem of continuous ink flow. Parker filled the barrel with an extraordinarily advanced threaded piston (an innovation that predated the Post syringe-type filling system by around eighty years and the Pelikan piston by about a century). It was sealed to prevent the ink from leaking out of the rear of the barrel and, most important, it metered the ink, preventing a vacuum in the barrel with a strand of cotton which ran from the ink reservoir to the slit in the nib.

Throughout the nineteenth century, inventors applied their minds to the question of how to create a continuous flow of ink by preventing the formation of a vacuum in the reservoir as soon as any ink was drawn to the nib. Mallet, a company in France, developed a tap on the side of the barrel (where the cock-lever had been on the Sheffer Pen-O-Graphic) in 1859, and Wirt, Mabie Todd, and Prince were also trying to prevent that vacuum, designing complex feeds or using variations on the spout.

But proper ink flow required the channeled feed, which was not invented until the late nineteenth century. The channeled feed meters ink flow to the paper and prevents the vacuum by passing air up the channel as the ink flows down it. More importantly, commercial production of working fountain pens became possible at the same time because techniques had been developed to produce large quantities of parts.

This brings us to Lewis Waterman's invention of 1882. Legend has it that Waterman, an insurance salesman, had an epiphany after accidentally spilling ink onto an insurance contract. No one is exactly clear as to how Waterman, who was

[1]

neither an inventor nor tinkerer, could have suddenly developed the intricate metering system of the channeled feed that eluded inventors for hundreds of years. Nevertheless in 1884, Lewis Waterman did start commercial production of reservoir pens using a channeled feed. So fountain pens,

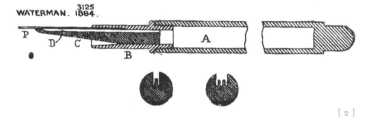

[2]

which had been in use in tiny quantities for a hundred years, became another beneficiary of mass-production, developed in the late nineteenth century.

Other companies soon put fountain pens into mass production and lured customers by advertising that they were making working fountain pens. This is why after supposedly "inventing" the mass-producible fountain pen, Waterman approached feed manufacturers. It is not clear who

[1]
Watermans eye-dropper in box, 1899, with instructions.
[2]
Lewis Waterman's Patent

these manufacturers were producing feeds for prior to Waterman's invention; quills, then in general use, had no need
for anything remotely resembling a feed. Numerous manufacturers of writing instruments (Mabie Todd, Paul Wirt,
John Holland, Prince, Mallet) had been experimenting
with different ways of getting reservoir pens to write, and

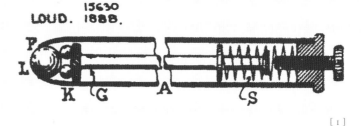

[1]

Paul Wirt even had patents going back to 1873 on various
aspects of the fountain pen. In addition, there had been patents for inventions resembling ballpoint pens since 1888
(Loud), which, given the tolerances needed to cause the ink
to flow and the need for oil-based ink, in all likelihood
didn't work.

[2]

[3]

[4]

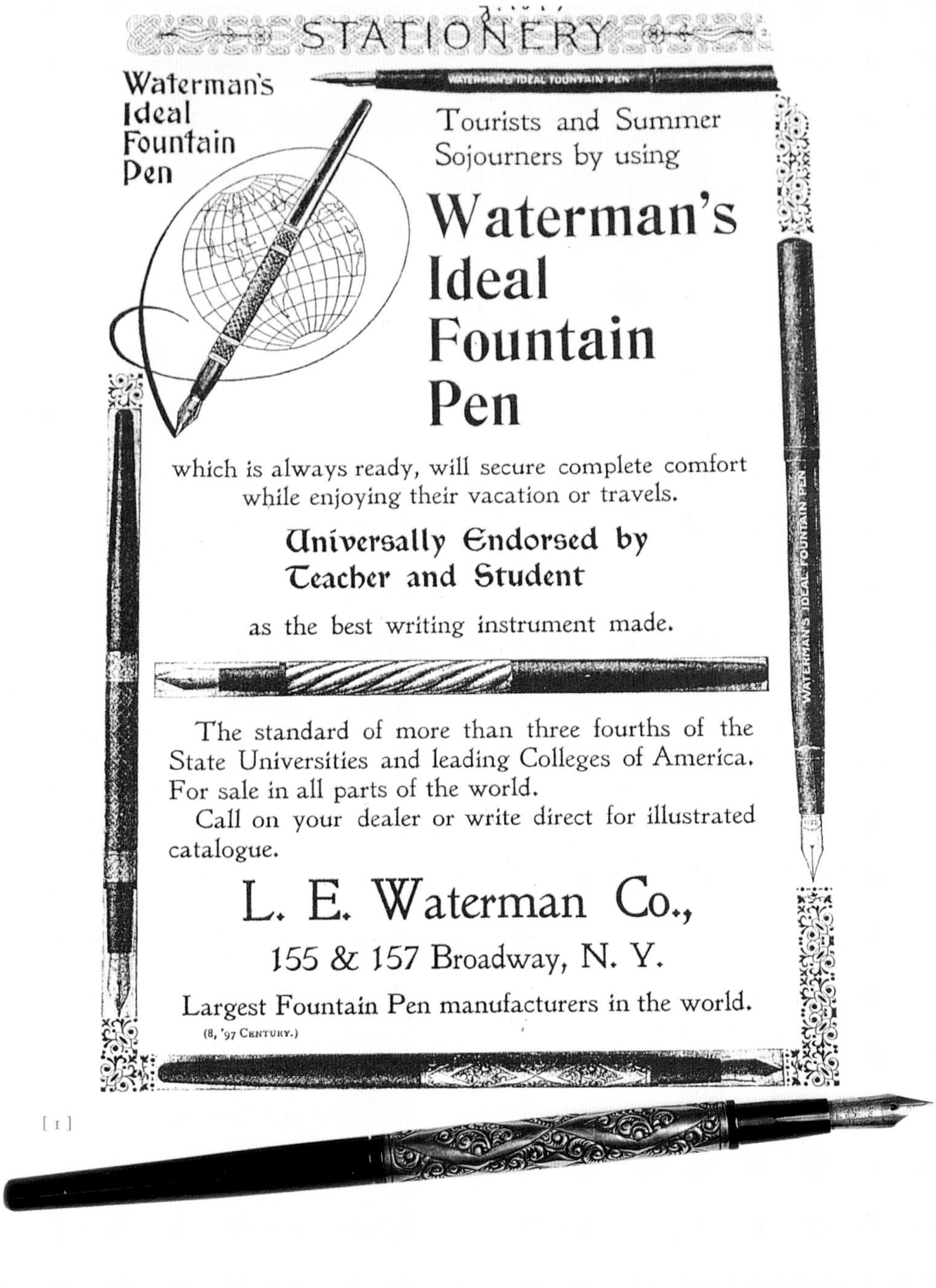

STATIONERY
WATERMAN'S IDEAL FOUNTAIN PEN
Waterman's Ideal Fountain Pen
Tourists and Summer Sojourners by using
Waterman's Ideal Fountain Pen
which is always ready, will secure complete comfort while enjoying their vacation or travels.
Universally Endorsed by Teacher and Student
as the best writing instrument made.
WATERMAN'S IDEAL FOUNTAIN PEN
The standard of more than three fourths of the State Universities and leading Colleges of America. For sale in all parts of the world.
Call on your dealer or write direct for illustrated catalogue.
L. E. Waterman Co.,
155 & 157 Broadway, N. Y.
Largest Fountain Pen manufacturers in the world.
(8, '97 Century.)

[1]

But at this early stage, the focus was on utility rather than appearance, and manufacturers were concentrating on getting their pens to write properly rather than look sophisticated. Even ten years later, when companies such as Parker were trying to make their names and develop fountain pens that wrote better than the competition's, the main effort was still directed toward function over appearance.

[1]
Waterman's eye-dropper pen with advertisement, 1890s.
[2]
Traveling eighteen-carat gold pen in fitted presentation box with owners' details, formerly belonging to the Duke of Wellington and presented by him in 1814. Made by renowned goldsmith Alexander J. Strachan with gold hallmark for 1800, this piece features a locking gold integral nib that slides out, a pencil holder mounted in a shaft with calibrated ruler, and an inkwell that slides out and unscrews to reveal a plug with a removable crosshatched wafer seal. On the end of the inkwell is the engraved seal of a nautical knot.

[2]

CHAPTER TWO

1880-1910: EARLY MARKETING EFFORTS

Once the function of the pen had been established, fountain pen companies began making their pens more attractive to increase their market share. First, companies made their pens look different from the competition; before that, all fountain pens—whether from Watermans, Parker, Paul Wirt, or Mabie Todd—had shared a similar look. They were of similar size, similar materials (hard rubber), and had similar caps and barrels. At that time, fountain pens sold well by establishing a reputation for performing better—not looking better—than the competition.

In the 1880s, the New York firm Mabie Todd had experimented with making the mechanicals look different and various, early distinctive Mabie Todd feeds can be found, but they are an exception. Mabie Todd tried making the pens in different colors, a difficult goal since they didn't control hard-rubber production. Their first attempts were merely black pens hand-

[1]
**Conklin No. 4 crescent-filler
in red-black mottled hard
rubber, 1903.**

[1]

painted with red to blend in with the black hard rubber. Soon all the pen companies wanted to use this new red and black coloring, so in the mid-1890s the rubber companies worked out how to use stable coloring in the high temperatures of hard rubber production to meet the companies' orders. By this time, Parker had started to give their pens a distinct twisted appearance or hexagonal shape. Soon companies started decorating barrels and caps with chasing, engine-turning, or elegant twist patterns and, during the 1890s, covering them with gold and silver or with panels of mother-of-pearl or abalone. Curiously however, most pens were still made in black and red. Only a very few pens in other colors have surfaced from this era (such as a sole Conklin crescent-filler from about 1903 and, slightly later, Parker button-fillers in green-blue mottled hard rubber), and these have been found only in individual examples.

Technologically, most pens were very similarly made. The exception is an inexpensive but extraordinarily advanced metal pen made by Eagle that appeared in the early 1890s and used a glass cartridge. Around 1900, companies started using more

Parker in green mottled hard rubber, 1910.

metal, at first with similar-looking metal bands around the hard rubber barrels. Companies also used mother-of-pearl panels to adorn the barrel between the metal bands. Around the same time, companies also began to overlay the barrel with intricate Art Nouveau filigree work in primitive styles, later working floral designs into the filigree as the taste for Art Nouveau changed.

As the pens started to look different from one another, companies experimented with making them self-filling. There were two false starts to this process. The first was the Eagle pen that used a glass cartridge. To keep the costs down, Eagle made the feed of poor quality and the nibs of an inexpensive base metal easily corroded by the acidity of normal ink and that quickly wore out. Many of these pens can be found today in mint condition with their cartridges intact, which seems to suggest that they weren't used all that much. This lack of use may have been because the inks designed for use in the then-prevalent quill pens tended to clog such a cheap feed. Any attempt to refill the cartridge would probably have resulted in a pen that no longer worked. The other false start was a late 1890s Watermans pump filler. This was a profoundly unsuc-

[2]

Kaweco gold-filled eyedropper with
inset diamonds, 1900.

Two similar filigrees pens, one
marked Watermans, the other
unmarked, ca. 1900. The same
metalwork companies made the filigree for most pen manufacturers.

Aikin Lambert crisscross
filigree eyedropper, 1910.

Aluminum Parker, 1897. This was an exceptionally expensive model because at the time of its introduction aluminum was nearly as precious as gold.

Conklin crescent-filler in black chased hard rubber. This No. 75 pen was the largest made by Conklin; 1914.

Watermans No. 2 pump-filler with silver-filigree main barrel, 1900s.

cessful pen with a design flaw: its barrel was open at both ends to a strong internal pump that created a gush of ink. The only way of knowing that the pen was full was when ink started spraying out all over the user's hands, clothes, insurance contracts, and so on.

After 1900, self-filling mechanisms began appearing. The first of these twentieth-century pens appear to have been the unusually named Self Fountain Pen. It had a rubber sack within the barrel that could be depressed by an extended "lever" running along the length of the barrel. The problem was that the pen tended to flood as it was difficult not to press the lever against the sack while writing. Although this design's patent was dated 1891, the pen itself did not appear in production until 1898, indicating the paucity in available self-filling designs.

The Wiedlich match-filler was the first widely available self-filling design. A sack in the pen's barrel was filled by pushing a matchstick into a hole on the side of the barrel; it was the precursor to the Conklin crescent-filler, which was the first commercial success in self-filling fountain pens. The Conklin used a large crescent-shaped protuberance sticking out of the side of the

[1]
Paillard Semper advertisement.

[1]
Onoto Semper advertisement.
[2]
Post filigree syringe-type filler.
Barrel with syringe in full position.
[3]
Onoto No. 8 piston filler in red-
black mottled hard rubber.

barrel to depress the sack when the crescent was not held in place by a locking ring. Like most other advances in pen technology, it was only a slight advance over what was otherwise available. Within a short period, more elegant—not to mention more obvious— ways of doing the same thing were patented. But the Conklin was indisputably successful and extraordinarily well distributed. It was available not only in its Ohio-based regional market but also all over the United States and Europe. Even eighteen-carat gold models were produced for distributors in France. Not only was the patented Conklin crescent-filler a worldwide success at a time when Watermans was recovering from their own failed pump-filler, it was actively imitated by more established competitors. Its influence was apparent when companies like Watermans not only didn't sue Conklin to prevent erosion of their own market share by this upstart self-filler, they even marketed their own version. Paul E. Wirt and Parker marketed their own versions of the crescent-filler with the click-filler. They tried to avoid the Conklin patent by

[1]

[2]

[3]

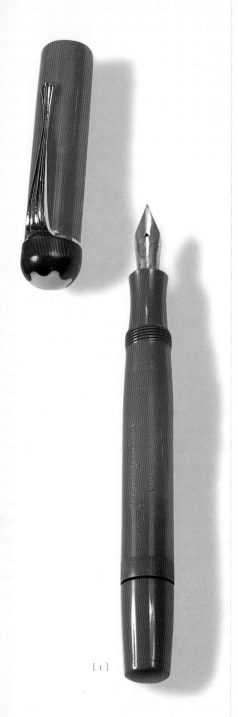

[1]

reshaping the crescent and putting the locking mechanism at the end of the barrel rather than at the side.

By the beginning of the twentieth century, self-filling designs took one of two forms. Alongside the mechanisms that held the ink in rubber sacks were the mechanisms that held a much larger ink supply within the barrel itself. The relatively widely distributed Post pen, which used a simple syringe in the barrel, was probably what inspired George Sweetser (a vaude-ville artist specializing in a transvestite act on roller skates) to invent the piston-filler. De La Rue's Onoto used a piston to create a vacuum inside the barrel. When released in an ink bot-tle, the vacuum drew the ink up into the barrel. This technol-ogy had first been used successfully by De La Rue and then by other companies in various forms for the next fifty years.

An equally important development was the Crocker blow-filler, which had a simple hole in the end of the barrel. In order to fill it, the nib was submerged in ink and the user blew through the hole into the barrel, causing the sack to deflate. When the sack reinflated, the vacuum pressure within the sack sucked up ink. This design (which was developed into the Chilton pneumatic filler mechanism and introduced around 1901) was so functional that it also was used in various forms for the next half century. Ultimately, in the form of the Sheaffer Snorkel of the 1950s, it married the sack-type mechanism with the piston type.

In the early twentieth century, the public began to demand greater facility in everyday implements. Fountain pens became easier to use with self-filling mechanisms and handier to hold. Parker's innovation in the latter regard was to add a clip on the side of the cap that held the pen upright in the pocket, ready for use. It also held the ink away from the joint where the section met the barrel and away from the feed and nib, thereby reducing leakage.

Parker's initial clip was the disappearing model: It operated as a clip when the barrel was placed in the cap; but when the pen was being used, it retracted and lay flush with the cap. It was, however, easily broken, so around 1908, Parker developed a pocket clip that installed quickly by simply unscrewing a blind cap and sandwiching the clip between the cap and blind cap. Soon, competitors such as Conklin, Swan, and Watermans were

[1]
Montblanc compressor filler.
[2]
1910 B & H Co. side button filler. This appears to have been an uncomfortable development of the Wiedlich Matchstick Filler.

[2]

[1]
Parker filigree showing disappearing clip, 1904.

[2]
Moore No. 85 improved safety showing VV clip. This unusual design features a nib that extended out of the barrel. On the "improved safety" pens, which appeared in 1911, the cap could be removed only when the barrel was grasped through the holes at the sides.

[3]
Parker snake pen showing VV clip. The top manufacturers adorned their best pens with the snake design. Such pens are very rare today and highly desired by collectors; 1905.

scurrying to find their own methods for achieving the popular feature that Parker was managing so easily.

At that time, companies wanting a clip had to buy a poor, complex, patented design. It required drilling holes in the cap and inserting the clip through those holes to rest between the cap and an internal blind cap, which had to be carefully manipulated into place over the attaching plates. All of these steps slowed production significantly and increased the costs. Even worse, the pen companies didn't control the patent to this clip and had to buy them from the manufacturer, Van Valkenburgh.

Although in some European markets clips weren't wildly popular (Swan and Montblanc managed to do without an integral clip for years), in the United States it became difficult to compete with Parker after 1908 in any market without some form of clip. For this reason, Conklin tried large numbers of clip designs before coming up with their own, somewhat stronger, Van Valkenburgh–type model. Watermans developed an exterior clip secured by two rivets that, although strong and practical, was just as complex and time-consuming to install.

[1]

[2]

[3]

CHAPTER THREE

Nobody familiar with the Standard Oil antitrust case of 1910 can see stifling of innovation and prevention of competition as problems new to the 1990s computer business. They even affected the fountain pen business. Litigious tendencies among pen producers posed a very real problem during the late nineteenth century that has never been studied particularly deeply. In particular, innovation tended to be stifled by Waterman's attempts to prevent anyone from competing with them in what they would have liked to have been their own sewn-up market.

In reality there wasn't one company in control of the market at any particular stage. In the mid-1890s, Paul Wirt was selling pens by the millions while Watermans was trying to sell by the tens of thousands. However, Watermans saw themselves as the premier pen company, possibly because it was based in New York and possibly because their founder, Lewis Waterman, owned

[1]
A.A. Watermans filigree, 1900.
[2]
Two Osmias, Pelikan bottle, and
Montblanc dummy in background.

the patents for the channeled feed. He readily sued anyone infringing those patents and was quite successful at it. An astute businessman, Waterman had registered patents while others had merely started producing pens.

By the first decade of the twentieth century, Watermans had scared most other pen manufacturers either into submission or into agreeing not to compete in markets where Watermans wanted a large market share. (This position contrasts markedly with the position in the 1990s, when, despite having been the pre-eminent name in quality pen production for most of the earlier part of the twentieth century, Watermans let any other company—even foreign companies—outspend them and create greater market share.) The competitors who coexisted more successfully with Watermans suggested that they weren't competing because they only distributed pens in a small regional market. Mabie Todd did this by concentrating their operations in Great Britain, where, for the ominous moment, Watermans was not competing. The British market was difficult, however, because De La Rue had developed their startlingly successful

[1]
Watermans
advertisement from
1919 highlighting the
much-published use of
one of their pens by
David Lloyd George to
sign the Treaty of
Versailles, bringing
World War I to an end.
[2]
Parker advertisement
from World War I.

Waterman's (Ideal) Fountain Pen

Aiding the world's greatest thinkers
to plan its greatest good

PARIS

Sold by Best
Dealers Everywhere

L.E. Waterman Company
191 Broadway, New York
CHICAGO · BOSTON · SAN FRANCISCO · MONTREAL · LONDON · PARIS · BUENOS AIRES

[2]

[1]
1910 Red-gold Onoto piston-filler.
[2]
1925 Montblanc dragonbox with No. 2L safety and ink bottle, each with rose band.

[1]

Onoto piston self-filling design there. This piston-filler was gaining preeminence all around the world, except in the United States. In certain countries such as Japan, De La Rue had a virtual monopoly on the market, and other companies wanting to compete had to produce a pen that looked like an Onoto. Although it was very difficult to compete with De La Rue, De La Rue was not prepared to take on Watermans on Waterman's home territory. Amazingly, when De La Rue opened their U.S. Onoto subsidiary on Fourth Avenue in New York City, they did so with the ink pencil, a stylographic eyedropper that virtually every other manufacturer had dropped as soon as the channeled feed was introduced.

Other companies competed with Watermans by being so new or small that Watermans wouldn't bother to take them on or by introducing truly innovative products that Watermans couldn't copy. In this way, a development came about that took Watermans and the other manufacturers completely unawares. In the early years of the twentieth century, a tiny new company called Sheaffer based in the wilds of Iowa developed a filling

mechanism which used a lever that lay flush with the side of the barrel. In use, it pressed onto a pressure bar that depressed the sack uniformly along its length. It was simple, attractive, and easy to use, and filling with the lever did not entail dismantling the pen, so the user was less likely to lose pieces.

The pen companies were in trouble: Watermans didn't have a self-filler that could compete, and Conklin's mechanism soon looked decidedly eccentric and ungainly when set against the Sheaffer lever. There were alternatives, but curiously enough, no one in the United States at that time thought to develop the Crocker design that used a vacuum in the barrel to deflate the sack. Although Montblanc would copy it with their compressor fillers, even they only sold such mechanisms in tiny numbers, primarily in France. Parker and Wirt concentrated on making versions of the Conklin less unwieldy.

The Crocker design was eventually developed—by Seth Crocker's son's company, Chilton—in the mid-1920s. Chilton refined the design by developing a sealed exterior tube outside the barrel, retaining the hole at the end that the Crocker had

[2]

[1]
From left:
John Holland filigree hatchet
filler, 1917;
Sterling silver Moore Safety in
repoussé design, 1903 ;
Early 1900s Watermans No. 224
"Indian Scroll" half-covered eye-
dropper in sterling silver with
taper cap.

used. By sliding the exterior tube back, covering the hole and pushing the tube back into position, air was expelled from the sack in exactly the same way as in the Crocker. The pen was then left in the ink, or the exterior tube pulled back out again with the hole covered to create another vacuum again for speed of filling, and the sack filled on reinflation.

But whereas the German company Montblanc freely copied others' ideas, the major American pen companies just didn't license other companies' designs (presumably because it would have been difficult to base a major national advertising campaign on someone else's idea) and their foreign subsidiaries approached the problem of how to compete with Sheaffer in two main ways. Parker tried to claim that their highly complex button-filler, which used multiple components to push the sack closed from the end rather than the side and which involved taking sundry bits off the pen in order to do so, was an equally good design. Alternatively, they used a lever that didn't look like a lever; John Holland, for example, introduced a hatchet-filler (which is, in reality, only a lever working inelegantly in

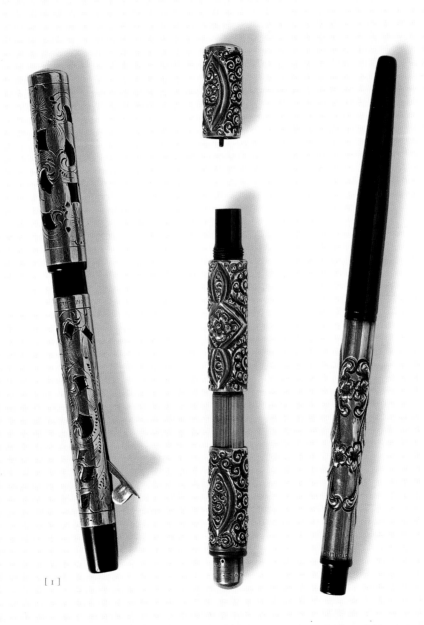

[1]

**Silver Astoria and Montblanc
safety pens. The Astoria factory
was set up by a former Montblanc
manager called Ilgner, in 1924.
Astoria produced high quality
pens which were similar to
Montblanc pens. In 1932, the
company was forced into bankruptcy by the Depression and was
taken over by Montblanc.
Thereafter, Astoria pens and nibs
could be found in Montblanc's
own catalogues.**

[2]

**Tibaldi Perfecta Automatica,
1927. The lever-filler was not the
only mechanism that was copied.
This unusual eyedropper filler
resembles a safety in which the nib
is permanently extended and is
held in place with a spring. The
eye-dropper itself pushes the nib
into the barrel and engages with a
tube to inject the ink into the pen.**

reverse) and clumsy saddle-fillers, which used a slightly less inelegant and less obstructive version of the crescent and purported to pull the sack full rather than use a lever to push it. Later on came the Aurora designs, which married the hatchet-filler to the button, and the curious Corona design, in which turning the blind cap acted on an internal pressure bar, depressing the sack.

Even less successful were the myriad companies, such as Century, Aikin Lambert, and Watermans whose pens used a hole in the side of the barrel to press a pressure bar. In fact, this idea was not so different from the early match-fillers.

[1]

In the early 1910s, Watermans tried a new competitive tactic with Sheaffer. They revived an eyedropper design called the
"Safety", dating back to the mid-1890s. A spiral inside the barrel retracted the nib into the barrel when not in use and held it
in the ink chamber. Watermans touted it as a "safety pen,"
emphasizing the huge reservoir and the leak-proof sealed ink-
chamber. (Swan, unlike Watermans, used the word safety to
mean that the cap screwed onto the barrel, rather than slip-fit,
so that it was supposedly safe from leaking.) The Watermans
Safety was relatively successful at first in all markets, but later
found its primary audience in Europe. Undoubtedly its success
was due, at least in part, to the fact that it could be marketed as
both new and different while essentially conservative. The United
States and Britain largely abandoned safety designs when self-
fillers gained hold of the market in the mid-1910s, but safety
pens were sold successfully in France, Germany, and Italy well
into the 1930s.

In the United States, the public wanted truly new things,
not just old ones promoted as new. Although the safety was

[2]

Europa pierced and engraved
two-tone spiral design safety
pen, mid-1930s.

Two unusual 1910s safety pens in
hard rubber: Onoto safety pen in
black and Swan safety pen in red
and black. Neither of these companies made many safety pens, and
in the case of Onoto, the safety is
almost unknown.

Italian Watermans No. 42
18KR safety pen, 1930s. The
cap depicts Aurora, a 1614
ceiling fresco by Guido
Reini, which is in the Casino
Rospiglioso, Palazzo
Pallavicini, Rome.

Montblanc No. 6 repoussé
gold-filled safety, ca. 1925.

Ladies 18KR Aurora safety
pen with female figure
applied to barrel.

Italian safety pen, 1920,
commemorating the country's victory
over Austria at the end of World War
I. Legend has it that the angel of god
appeared over the boats of the Italian
soldiers as they crossed the river
Piove, on their way to decisively
defeating the Austrians.

Early 1930s 18KR Watermans No: 42
safety pen depicting Titian's "Sacred
and Profane Love" (1514, Borghese
Gallery, Rome) around the cap, while
the barrel shows a Roman sculpture
called Cupid and Psyche. Original in
the Villa Farnesina, Rome.

Montblanc No. 6L safety
Montblanc No. 00 Baby long
safety, teardrops pattern in
900 grade silver, 1920s.

Montblanc silver lily of the
valley pattern safety pen.

1920s Kaweco 900 grade
silver niello baby safety pen
often referred to as 00 size
in floral design.

Williamson black chased hard rubber sleeve-filler, 1910. Looking like a Moore's safety pen, this pen has a fixed nib and is filled by means of the sleeve under the barrel end. Williamson was a small company based in Turin, Italy.

Montblanc safety pens in silver.

[1]
Dunhill advertisement.
[2]
Watermans No. 418 PSF sleeve-filler, 1915.
[3]
Watermans No. 418 PSF sleeve-filler in silver filigree, 1915.

selling relatively well, pen companies still needed something that could compete with Sheaffer. Thus in the mid-teens they reacted with a number of designs, principally coin-fillers and sleeve-fillers (essentially variations on the matchstick filler), which were, however, unsuccessful and lasted only a short period.

Early sleeve-fillers were as bulky and ungainly as the decades-old Conklin crescent. The sleeve interfered with writing and ruined the balance of the pen. It also reduced the ink supply by taking up too much space inside the barrel. These sleeve-fillers were the pen companies' last gasp attempt to compete with Sheaffer's lever pen. After that, pen companies concentrated production around a lever within a box section or a lever held in with an internal metal ring. These variations apparently didn't conflict with Sheaffers patent.

Parker was slow to advance technologically and didn't feel the need to hype their inferior self-fillers until they were forced to do so by Sheaffer's success. They responded by finally introducing

[1]

[2]

[3]

Meteore advertisement.

SPHÉRO-MÉTÉORE

Syste Jean Petx
Breveté S.G.D.G.

UN CADEAU
TOUT TROUVÉ
ET FLATTEUR

UNE ŒUVRE
ARTISTIQUE
ET UN ARTICLE
UTILITAIRE

LE SPHÉRO-MÉTÉORE
EST DE CONCEPTION
ENTIÈREMENT
FRANÇAISE

B. MARIC
STUDIO MÉTÉORE

PAPETERIE - GRAVURES
MUSIQUE

LIBRAIRIE M. LIVRAGHE
28, Avenue de Tourville
PARIS VII° R. C. Seine 72.371

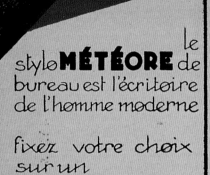

le stylo **MÉTÉORE** de bureau est l'écritoire de l'homme moderne

fixez votre choix sur un

SPHÉRO·MÉTÉORE

ses socles artistiques vous charmeront et sa fabrication française est impeccable.

their button filler, which they had patented in 1904. At that time, they were experimenting with self-fillers without the urgency of needing to compete with Sheaffer. Their first attempt to make a self-filler was that click-filler based on a short-lived Wirt design, with their own version of the protuberance that sticks out of the barrel and depresses the sack. But, eventually, Parker settled on the button-filler, claiming that a button under a removable blind cap at the end of the barrel exerting longitudinal pressure on a sprung pressure bar within the barrel, which in turn springs into the sack, was some type of innovation.

MATERIALS

Around the 1920s, pens were also changing in appearance as the rubber companies worked out how to use bright colors that would remain stable in the high temperatures involved in hard rubber production. Pen companies then started to use these colored materials to make pens. European companies like Mabie Todd and De La Rue, in England, and Montblanc (including Rouge et Noir and the various sub-brands made by Excelsior)

[1]

[2]

[3]

FROM the falling water's rainbow-tinted mists and the radiant ripples of the sunlit mountain pool came the inspiration for these alluring two-tone Ripple Rubber Waterman's.

There are color values that only ripples can express in these new Ripple-Blugreen, Ripple-Rose and Ripple-Olive fountain pens.

The fact that these pens are made of stainless rubber, light and resilient, is added assurance that they will satisfy.

Ask at the nearest Waterman's dealer to see all three colors in two sizes. There are pencils to match.

PRICES
All Colors

Large pen $5.00
Short pen $4.00

Pencils to match
$2.00 and $1.50

Waterman's

[1]

and Kaweko, in Germany, were reluctant to interfere with conservative colors and continued producing the vast majority of their pens in black. But U.S. companies, which had had success with the earlier mottled rubber, developed a somewhat redder "woodgrain" appearance. These, in turn, gave way to a predominantly red ripple design.

Famously, Parker very tentatively introduced a bright red color for its successful Lucky Curve pen, which had been produced in black up to the early 1920s. They initially produced only a handful of pens in red that weren't salesman's samples, but immediately the "big red" and its Duofold family were wildly successful and easily outstripped other Parker productions in all but the lowest-end pens. To keep up, Sheaffer introduced brightly colored high-end pens, initially in hard rubber and, later, in their version of celluloid.

Numerous companies experimented with colored pens in extraordinary ways. They used highly inflammable nitro-cellulose. They also tried casein, a milk product, in the 1920s. Although casein, curiously, is being tried again today, it never really caught

[2]

on in the 1920s because it tended to degrade or break. Casein absorbs moisture from the atmosphere and swells, then contracts when it dries, wreaking havoc with tolerances. Cracks that developed after this process had happened a few times were very common. Eventually, the pen companies settled on celluloid, a plastic that had been commonly used since the mid-1890s by filmmakers. Sheaffer called it Radite, Parker called it Permanite, Wahl-Eversharp called it Pyralin. As the 1930s progressed, these celluloid pens included a particularly beautiful and, today, collectable material made by Bayer that they boldly called Bayer Celluloid. It was used by Montblanc, Omas, and others.

[1]

LeBoeuf, an unknown company in Springfield, Massachusetts, was the first pen manufacturer to recognize the potential of celluloid. In 1919, they patented a way of making pens out of tubing, rather than drilled-out rod stock, and the patent actually shows celluloid tubing being used! This was revolutionary because it was six years before other major companies started using any plastics. However, as so often happened, there is no evidence that LeBoeuf actually manufactured any pens before the mid-1920s, and most of their exceptionally beautiful pens come from the late 1920s to early 1930s.

WARRANTIES

By the mid-1920s, a new marketing problem appeared on the horizon for the major pen companies. Sheaffer hit on the idea of introducing a lifetime warranty on what had always been an exceptionally well-made and reliable handmade product. Sheaffer found that by doing this, it could increase both sales and the sale price to cover potential returns under that warranty. It saw that if lifetime warranties were offered, many people wouldn't

[2]

Die Renaissance der Farbe ~ ~

Füllhalterständer mit einem Einstecker einschliesslich Verlängerer von Mk. 21,– bis Mk. 40,–

Der Parker Duofold ist eine Kostbarkeit fürs Leben

Nach einer Zeit, in der die Buntheit fast als unvornehm verpönt war, bekennen wir uns jetzt wieder freudig zum reizvollen Spiel der Farben. Wo Sie auch hinblicken, in der Ausstattung unserer Wohnungen, in der lichten Kleidung unserer Damen, überall zeigt sich Ihnen die „Renaissance der Farbe". Und Sie haben es schon oft erlebt und erleben es immer wieder aufs neue, wie lichte und farbenfrohe Umgebung und Gerätschaften Ihre Phantasie beflügeln und die geistige Schöpferkraft und Arbeitsfreude beleben und steigern. Parker stellt den Reiz der Farbe in seinen Dienst. Er denkt an Ihren Schönheitssinn und den wohltuenden Einfluss warm-leuchtender Farben und hat Künstler berufen, die für den Parker Duofold ein herrliches Gewand entwarfen.

Chinesisch Lackrot, die Farbe einer Jahrtausende alten Kultur, Lapislazuliblau, die Farbe des Steins, aus dem die Ägypter ihre heiligen Skarabäen schnitten, Jadegrün, die Farbe des Jadesteins, Mandaringelb, die heilige Farbe des „Sohnes des Himmels", und die satte Farbe des Jett geben den Parker-Haltern einen eigenen Reiz. Mit der Kultur des Geschmacks vereint sich im Parker Duofold höchste technische Vollendung. Leicht liegt er in der Hand, gleichmässig fliesst die Tinte schon bei der „drucklosen Berührung". Die Osmiridium-Federspitze zeigt noch nach jahrzehntelangem Gebrauch keine Abnutzung, die Hülse ist unzerbrechlich. Schnell und bequem füllen Sie den Parker direkt aus der Tintenflasche.

Gehen Sie in das nächste einschlägige Geschäft und versuchen Sie in einer Schreibprobe selbst, wie leicht und angenehm der Parker Duofold schreibt. Der Händler wird sich freuen, Ihnen Gelegenheit zu diesem Versuch geben zu dürfen.

Füllhalterständer mit zwei Einsteckern einschliesslich Verlängerern von Mk. 38,– bis Mk. 85,–

35 Mk **30** Mk **25** Mk **20** Mk

Parker Duofold

PARKER A.-G., HEIDELBERG-DOSSENHEIM

want to buy pens without such warranties. Then Sheaffer found that they could dramatically reduce warranty repairs by increasing the amount of gold in the nib and making it very rigid. This change would largely prevent breakages, which occurred commonly with flexible nibs.

The warranty was effective and its influence rippled outward quickly. When the directors of Montblanc came to the United States on one of their regular trips, in 1925, to see what current ideas they could use in Germany, they learned of the lifetime warranty and have been using its outward appearance ever since. They designated their pens covered by a lifetime warranty "Meisterstück," which they then exported all over the world, often using the local language to specify the warranted pens—Chef D'Oeuvre in France, Capolavoro in Italy, and Masterpiece in Great Britain. This use of "Masterpiece" to designate an extended warranty continued until the postwar period when Montblanc began injection-molding their pens. Because injection-molded pens weren't particularly durable, it was difficult to continue offering an extended warranty. In true American fashion, this

[2]

[1]
Kaweco No. 2, 900-grade silver niello safety pen and matching traveling ink bottle.

German company responded to that marketing challenge by heavily promoting the supposed precision of their injection-molding techniques.

Throughout the late 1920s and early 1930s, in order for other major pen manufacturers, including Parker, Watermans, and Eversharp, to compete with Sheaffers' lifetime warranty, they had to increase marketing spending, constantly introduce new models and materials, and try technological advances to maintain market share. The result was that these companies sold only slightly greater numbers of an ever-increasing multitude of models. Moreover, there just weren't the technological advances to warrant changing the models. However, as Depression gripped countries where people didn't have the money to fire the companies' sales, new models weren't necessarily what the public wanted. Eventually, most major companies were forced to offer extended warranties, which Parker did with its Blue Diamond line, Eversharp with its Gold Seal, Swan with its Eternal, and even Conway Stewart with its Duro.

[1]

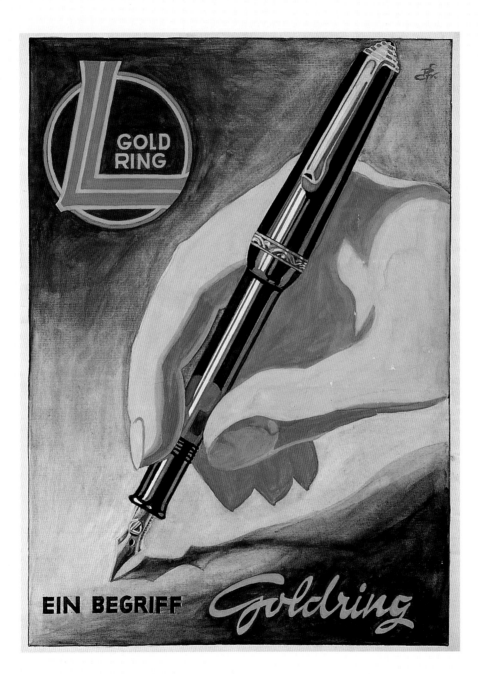

CHAPTER FOUR

1930-1940: HOW THE DEPRESSION
AFFECTED THE MARKET

By the 1930s the world was in the grips of the Great Depression. The public wanted to be daz-zled by technological marvels to take their minds off their economic woes. Hence the uncom-mon popularity of the Schneider Trophy seaplane races and the land-speed record attempts.

For fountain pen design, the Great Depression made utilitarianism and functionality the order of the day. As with architecture, in pen design, fashion dictated that the general impression created by the whole was a more up-to-date notion than interest in minutiae of detail in the constituent parts.

Pen manufacturers, who had been producing slightly bland mass-produced design, rec-ognized the popular mood and responded by trying to take technological leaps forward. Although they advertised new pens as breakthroughs, in reality materials weren't necessarily

[1]
Eversharp Coronet in green with a gold-filled cap, 1936. The Coronet was one of the Eversharp models to feature the ill-fated ink shut-off valve that caused the company so much trouble.
[2]
Swan display of pens, 1920s.

[1]

at a stage when the end product would benefit from any technological leaps.

Against this background, Wahl-Eversharp introduced the ink shut-off mechanism in a blaze of publicity. It was supposed to seal the ink supply shut when the cap was screwed onto the barrel, thereby preventing leakage, especially in aircraft. But despite the hype, the ink shut-off didn't work. After hundreds of thousands had been sold, the Federal Trade Commission noticed, and Wahl-Eversharp were prevented from further advertising it. As a result, manufacturers were forced to go back to the old eyedropper safety pens that they had been making since the early part of the century. Eyedropper models contained the ink within a sealed chamber so they couldn't leak even under pressure changes. Watermans soon dubbed their version "Aero-Waterman," and hailed it as a wonderful invention, but in reality they were the old safety designs in a slightly newer form.

With all pen designs up to this point, the user could not see how much ink was left in the reservoir, and most companies

[2]

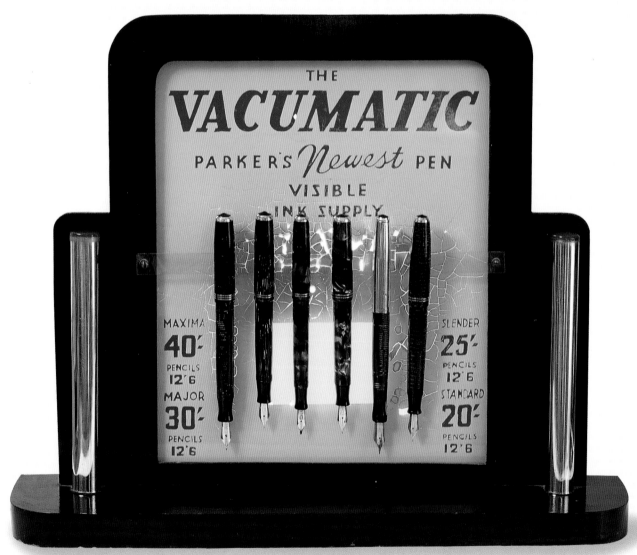

[1]
Parker Vacumatic display, 1932.
[2]
Parker Vacumatic Golden Web,
1932.

wanted to find a way to make the remaining ink supply visible. But such an advance was difficult with existing materials.

The only way to achieve this in the 1930s was to make the barrel material somewhat transparent, then drill out a hollow core, and hope that the shell would be strong enough to do the job. But this precluded the use of a sack and consequently was only possible with a piston-filling pen. Either the transparent section became too brittle or it reacted with the other material in the barrel-making it unstable. De La Rue had been using pistons successfully for more than thirty years, but most American companies were so devoted to the sack in its various forms that they had not yet copied the piston.

Eventually, Parker developed the Vacumatic filling system designed around an air-breather tube in the barrel. They replaced the sack with a diaphragm—or repositioned the sack horizontally at the end of the barrel, depending on which way you look at the development. The barrel was still drilled out, but this time it was made of layers of plastic; col-

[2]

Faber-Castell adver-
tisement for button-
filler pen and box,
1950. Faber-Castell
was called A. W. Faber
until the mid-1930s,
when their pens came
to be known as Faber-
Castell after the fami-
ly that owned the com-
pany. They seem to
have been unconnect-
ed to the Johann Faber
pen company that
made pens in New
York in the late nine-
teenth century.

Nach der Gold... Teil eines guten Fü... ist das Schriftbild abhängi... Für den *CASTELL*-Füllhalter wu... derer Tintenleiter konstruiert und ge... Große **Auffang-Kammern** nehmen die ... regulieren ihren Ausfluß je nach Schreibdruck. Das schöne, klare und gleichmäßige Schriftbild, das de... *CASTELL* besonders auszeichnet, ist darauf begründet. Auch das Klecksen wird durch diese großen Reserve-kammern verhindert.

...halter ...gefüllt. ...t kon-...tz Raum ...n Tinten-...ssungsver-...gt 2,5 ccm *CASTELL* ...wird sehr ge-scha... ...ie erhöht seinen Gebrauchswert.

1/448. 36. AR. I.

[1]
Quail advertisement

ored plastic was interspersed with transparent plastic so that the ink supply would show. Eventually, even Sheaffer caught up with the need for these technological developments and decided they had to introduce new technologies. When many other companies were going over to the trusty old lever-filler to simplify production and reduce costs (Parker with their Parkette line; even De La Rue introduced a lever-filler and Sager somewhat mysteriously introduced a lever-filler with the word sackless still imprinted on the barrel), Sheaffer was developing a piston-filler that would let the ink show through the barrel without there being a rubber sack in the way. Actually, this technique was quite an elegant way of doing things, as Sheaffer discovered something that De La Rue had known for quite some time: A piston design allowed virtually the whole barrel to be used for ink. Such a design removed, at last, the various filler parts that took up space within the barrel, increasing the ink supply.

The piston did have a problem, however. Whereas the sack was exceptionally easy to repair, the piston had a very precise

Quail

Sicherheits-Füllfederhalter

Marken:
Quail Domino
Quail Ideal
Quail Patriot
Quail Middle Joint

Unübertroffen

Alleinverkauf:

M. ERLEBACH Nachf. FRANKFURT a/M

[1]

size and fit and was quite difficult to replace. Repairers had to keep large supplies of varying sizes of precision-fitting piston-seals: Again, unless you use the infra-dig Onoto system with its easily removable piston, it is difficult replacing a seal on a piston. So difficult, in fact, that companies like Conklin made their cork piston permanent. In theory, the cork could not be replaced; but in practice, after the company went out of business, repairers found ways to replace that cork.

The transparent reservoir notwithstanding, many of the 1930s technological advances were not great breakthroughs and were quickly abandoned. Watermans and Swan, in fact, were forced by 1940s wartime shortages to discard most of their complex 1930s marvels. They and others rediscovered that the lever (or similar) pushing a pressure bar and depressing the sack was not such a bad idea after all, and continued to use it into the middle of the century. Parker went even further back for their postwar developments. They introduced the aerometric-filler in the 1950s on the 51 line. When the outer sleeve of the barrel was unscrewed, a semi-exposed sack

[1]
Soennecken Rheingold black and pearl "paddle"-filler, 1935. The Rheingold was a famous train of the 1930s, and the cap crown of this pen was designed to resemble the train front.
[2]
Swan lever-filler in fourteen-carat hand-engraved design.

[2]

[1]
Swam advertisement.
[2]
Watermans advertisement.

How to choose an *exclusive* Xmas Gift

Go to a "Swan" Fountpen dealer and from the wide variety of models, ranging from 10/6 up to £10, choose the pen you judge most suitable. Then choose the nib to suit your friend's hand—this can be pretty accurately decided by the sight of some handwriting. To complete, have your friend's name or an inscription neatly engraved on the pen. Thus, you will have chosen an exclusive Xmas Gift, because it is in every way adapted to that one particular individual.

Safety Pattern, with Screw-on Cap, from **12 6** up.

Standard Pattern, with Slip-on Cap, from **10/6** up.

"SWAN" FOUNTPENS

Sold Everywhere by Stationers and Jewellers.

Nibs to Suit Every Hand.

ENGRAVING ON "SWAN" PENS.
A touch of individuality is added to the gift of a "SWAN" Pen by having a name, initial, or monogram engraved upon it.

Charge :— 1/- for six letters or

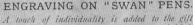

less, and 2d. per letter over six.

Write for Illustrated Catalogue.

Mabie, Todd & Co., Ltd.
79 & 80, High Holborn, W.C.
38, Cheapside, E.C.; 95a and 204, Regent Street, W., London; 3, Exchange Street, Manchester.
London Factory—319-329 Weston Street, S.E.
Paris, Zurich, Sydney, Toronto, &c.
Associate House—Mabie, Todd & Co., Inc., New York and Chicago.

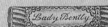

No war-time advance in prices of "Swan" Pens.

Before buying a fountain pen ask what its price was before the war ; don't pay 20 % advance for nothing.

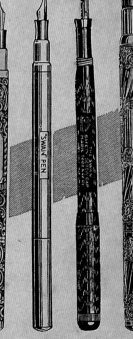

Size 3c.—Safety pattern full-covered silver, **40/-**

Size 1.—Standard pattern, slip-on cap, **10/6**

Size 1.—With two 18ct. rolled gold bands, **14 6**

Size 1.—Barrel covered chased silver, **27/6**

Size 1.—Full-covered rolled gold, **45/-**

Size 1.—Full-covered silver, **32/-**

Size 1.—Full plain silver, **12/6**

Size 3.—Full-covered chased silver, **52/6**

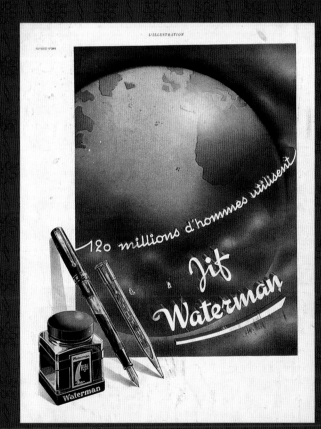

[1]
Conklin medium-sized lever-
filler in streaked green-white celluloid, 1930s.
[2]
Rare Pelikan model 100 pens
from the mid-1930s.

[1]

and pressure bar were exposed. The aerometric bore more than a passing resemblance to the sleeve-filler dating back to the mid-1910s.

There was an even more fundamental problem during this period for the pen companies in the 1930s. Pens had always been made by drilling out rod stock, initially in hard rubber and by the end of the 1920s, in plastic under its various commercial names. However, during the 1930s, pen companies introduced vast ranges of materials in various sizes to accommodate both their new designs and their older pens in traditional materials. This demand for variety required each company to maintain huge stocks of rods in numerous sizes and materials. But the rods in new plastics had to sit for lengthy periods while the material cured. In times of depression, financing this huge stock of rods was a major problem, so American pen companies set up one shared company to hold rod stock while it was curing. As a result, pens from different companies turn up in the same materials. For example, the plastic that Watermans' rare and desirable Patrician pens

Elmo senior-sized unusual
piston-filler in green-gold
marbled plastic, late 1930s.

1935 Green Columbus Extra 98.

Aska button-filler, mid-1930s. This extraordinarily beautiful and well-made pen was marketed
by this Swiss company and featured a gold-filled
Deco band around the cap lip between two silver
bands. Although marked FABRICATION SUISSE,
the company made primarily low-end fountain
pens and this one seems to have been made for
Aska by an Italian company, probably Nettuno.

Macniven & Cameron No. 2 "Waverley Golden Medal" lever-filler in red-striated silver pearl, 1930s. This Depression-era pen was made in low-grade plastic and created out of tubing rather than drilled-out rod stock. Although generally in good condition, the thin material has visibly contracted slightly over the ring that holds the lever in place inside the barrel.

Aurora Novum platinum-lined hatchet-filler with typical Aurora locking clip, late 1930s.

Triad, 1932. This unusual lever-filler from Rhode Island was triangular in section and had a locking mechanism in which the crown was unscrewed to release the cap from the barrel.

DE MEEST POPULAIRE
SERIE Nr 3 (HEEREN MODEL)
en 3V (KORT DAMESMODEL)
met verchroomd montuur

Nr 3
Grijsparel

Nr 3V
Wijnrood

Fl. 10.50

Fl. 10.50

Fl. 10.50

Bijpassende vulpotlooden Nr 93
à Fl. 4.50

Andere kleuren :
ZWART GLAD
ZWART PAREL
GROEN PAREL
N. B. — Wijnrood alleen in Damesmodel

NIEUW !...
DE JUNIOR PEN
met verchroomd montuur

Glad
Zwart

Licht
Blauw

Fl. 8.50

Bijpassende vulpotlooden à fl. 3.—

Andere kleuren :
BRUIN PAREL
DONKER BLAUW
DONKER GROEN

SERIE 92 (HEEREN MODEL)
en 92V (DAMES MODEL)
met verguld montuur

Drie nieuwe, zeer sprekende
kleuren in slangenhuid

Nr 92
Grijs Slangenhuid

Nr 92V
Bruin
Slangenhuid

Fl. 12.—

Fl. 12.—

Bijpassende vulpotlooden Nr 91
à Fl. 4.50

Andere kleuren :
ZWART GLAD
GROEN SLANGENHUID
GROEN GOUD
ROOD GOUD

NIEU
DE LADY PATRICIA D
met verchroomd montuur ; voor
vulpen wi

3 kleuren :

Grijs Parel

Bijpassende Vul

KLEUREN IN DE
LADY PATRICIA à FI

ZWART GLAD —
EMERALD — PERS

« WATERMAN » is de betrouwbaarste vulpen. De 14 karaats goude

R VULPENNEN

V !...

RZICHTIG à Fl. 15.—

ames, die ook een doorzichtige
bezitten.

d

Zwart Parel

SERIE 94
(ALLEEN HEEREN MODEL)

Mosgroen

Potlood 95

JUBILEUM PENNEN
Nr 5 & 7
Alleen in git-zwart

N. B. Nr 5, zelfde model als Nr 94
Verchroomd montuur Fl. 14.50
Potlood Nr 95 idem   Fl. 8.50

Nr 7
verguld
montuur

Potlood 97
id.

PATRICIAN

Een schitterend luxe-model
met groote, zeer solide
gouden pen

Onyx

Patrician
Potlood

Fl. 9.—

Fl. 9.—

Fl. 16.50

Fl. 17.50

Fl. 14

Fl. 26.50

ooden Fl. 8.50

ROEGERE SERIE

4.— (niet doorzichtig)

YX — TURQUOISE
— PAARLEMOER

Andere kleuren :

ZWART GLAD
BRUIN
} Verguld montuur

GRIJSPAREL
BLAUW
} Verchroomd montuur

7 Standaardpunten, door kleur aangeduid
op het ondereinde van den houder, waar-
van de 4 meest courante zijn :

BRUIN : Fijn en zacht.
ROSE } Fijn, zacht en zeer soepel, spe-
ciaal voor snelschrift.
ROOD : Medium 2, breeder dan fijn.
BLAUW : Een weinig schuin afgeslepen punt

Andere kleuren :

ZWARTGLAD — MOSGROEN
EMERALD — TURQUOISE
met verguld montuur.

PAARLEMOER met verchroomd montuur.

met zuiver iridium getipte pen, gaat een MENSCHENLEEFTIJD mee

[1]
Watermans advertisement from
Dutch (previous spread)
[2]
Goldring advertisement.
[3]
Examples of Eversharp materials
and nib styles, 1930s.

are made from is the same as that for Parker's inexpensive "Moderne" line sold during the Depression. A very popular black and gold plastic can be found in many manufacturer's lineups in exactly the same form.

Attempts to get away from this system in which a jointly owned and financed company held the stocks while they were curing can be seen in unusual and not always successful lines of pens from a few manufacturers. Sheaffer was never a part of this joint venture, so their pens tended to have a distinctive look. Wahl-Eversharp, which was a part of the consortium, used stocks from different sources such as the material used for their Doric line of pens. It isn't clear whether the Doric line of materials was in fact part of the consortium stock, but much of the Doric stock is positively unstable, and breaks easily.

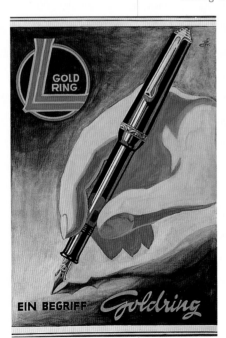

[2]

[3]

CHAPTER FIVE

1945: THE WAR: HOW BARGAIN
DEBASEMENT NURTURED THE BALLPOINT PEN

World War II was worse than the Depression for pen development. When the world became engulfed by war, fountain pen production took a back seat to war production. This had two immediate effects: First, government restrictions meant that the pen companies couldn't get the materials they needed to maintain pen production at commercial levels. This lack of supplies led to the development of various nibs made with significantly smaller amounts of gold, like the Parker 51, the Aurora 88, and various Omas pens that featured minuscule hooded nibs. Even worse, pen companies began manufacturing nibs out of base metals. This dire situation even affected luxury-market companies such as Montblanc, whose pens used tin nibs, made under their own name or marked Degussa.

Second, most of the pen companies' sophisticated production capacity was taken up with war production, and this didn't mean manufacturing pens for the military, which could only

use so many fountain pens. Companies with substantial facilities, such as Sheaffer, crossed over to making bomb sights for
military aircrafts. Companies such as Parker and Sheaffer
did, however, manage to get contracts from the military for
small amounts of fountain pens and thus continued to fill
some consumer demand.

But pen companies with proper management and reputations to protect, by and large, did not want to destroy those
reputations by producing pens using just any materials, especially when they had wartime contracts with which to pay their
staff. A void was thus created in the market as pens wore out
or were lost and consumers couldn't buy quality fountain
pens to replace them.

The stage was set for companies like Wearever to step in
and flood the American market with poorly produced tin-
nibbed pens made from low-quality materials produced
under ultra high-quantity, ultra low-cost military contracts.
As bad as these offerings were, they were all that consumers
could buy. The quality of these wartime plastics is obvious

[1]

Montblanc cat with original dummy pen.

[1]
Watermans advertisement
[2]
**Watermans desk stand with duck
and green marbled desk pen.**

from the way the pens distort with time and slight heat. The plastic barrels and caps often shrink around their internal metallic components. Things in other countries were even worse for consumers of fountain pens. Most German pen production was destroyed when the country's industrial facilities were bombed. Japanese companies were suffering from all these ills and more. Japanese fountain pens had always lagged behind the rest of the world technologically, but with war production being of preeminent importance, research and production of pens faced serious setbacks. Now, with so many former factory employees enlisted, rubber production, for example, ground to a halt.

Against this backdrop of the introduction of stiff nibs, years of poor-quality pens, and greatly decreased availability, an insidious development grabbed the pen market. The supposedly all new ballpoint could trumpet its technological virtues to a market eager to look at what it had to offer.

[1]

It is generally accepted knowledge that the fountain pen couldn't compete against the ballpoint when it was introduced, but the perceived wisdom has more pertinent explanations. The situation paralleled the postwar political situation in England when the governing party was thrown out as soon as victory in the war looked certain. People voted Churchill out of office at the end of World War II, not because they didn't appreciate him as a wartime leader or they didn't want him as prime minister, but because they remembered how poorly Churchill's party had done when in office before the war. In the same way, few would have embraced the ballpoint pen quite so strongly if they had been able to get hold of plentiful supplies of high quality, stylish and reasonably priced fountain pens. The ballpoint pen had a tip which strayed all over the paper and was difficult to control, making handwriting look terrible. The pens flooded and the oil-based ink couldn't be blotted up easily or at all. The ink tended to soak through the paper, so that only one side could be used. And although manufacturers

[I]
Dunhill-Namiki boxed set of eighteen pens, seventeen of which have decorated barrels and one of which is plain, ca. 1930. The purpose of this set was for the company artists to use design reference according to different requests with designs by different artists. Featuring work by Shogo, Toho, Shozan, Ei, Hiseki, Shisen, Shorin, Shohmi, and Seihoh.

[1]
Montblanc 246 piston-filler
lined with a platinum-like material, late 1940s to mid 1950s.
This material is highly prized by
collectors even though the 246
model was part of a line that was
not regarded as the highest quality
when new, and wasn't covered by
the lifetime warranty of the 142-
146 model.

Pelican and girl for Pelikan.

weren't mentioning it, there was no easy way to refill the
cartridge when the ink supply ran out. When touting a technological marvel, it is probably better not to tell anyone
that the new marvel is in fact a throwaway item.

But the new ballpoints were competing not with the
finest fountain pens, but with the cheaply made Wearevers.
Making matters worse, the old-line pen companies weren't
able to comprehend this point and for the most part didn't
accept that the ballpoint was there to stay. Once the war was
over, they tried to capture a greater market share by flooding
the market (not to mention the paper) with poorly made,
dreadfully designed pens, debasing both the quality of their
pens and their reputations. Having spent the first half of the
century telling the world about the quality of their pens, they
felt that the time had come when they could rely on hype
without providing quality. Using this hype, management
found that they could make huge profits, which increased
exponentially as the companies moved relentlessly downhill
in quality. In short, the pens got worse but the marketing

[2]

PLEXICOLOR
MALLAT

[1]
Mallat advertisement.
[2]
1948 Columbus Model 32
lever filler.

and the hype got better.

This marketing approach generally resulted in bankruptcy. The company was then taken over by one of its competitors who were themselves still at an earlier stage in the cycle or by one of its overseas subsidiaries, and the new owners realize that they cannot achieve high enough sales to revive the company without reviving the quality image.

Conklin and Chilton tried this product debasement technique in the 1930s—without the constraints of the wartime supply situation—and went bust. Watermans then tried debasing its products in the late 1940s, and this debasement resulted in a catastrophic sales slump. Watermans was driven into such financial straits that it had to be taken over by its French subsidiary. Eversharp tried the same tactic in the 1950s and was met by the same results, driving the company into a takeover by Parker, the sole purpose of which was to remove a competitor from the marketplace. Parker in turn tried product debasement in the 1960s, although they never actually stopped producing quality pens, they just stopped mass marketing them. Eventually, Parker was

[2]

[I]

Minerva celluloid button-filler in gray flame.

[I]

taken over by its U.K. subsidiary.

All in all, the willingness to accept new ideas which had made the United States fountain pen industry world leaders in the first half of the twentieth century was what (assisted by blinkered management and a heavy dose of short-termism) pushed it virtually off the map in the second half. All supposedly in response to the onslaught of the ballpoint.

Interestingly, in countries where commercialism didn't have quite so strong a hold, the supposedly unbeatable ballpoint pen wasn't so successful. In post-World War II Germany, companies like Montblanc restarted production with high-quality pens as soon as their factories were in production again and until they, in turn, started widespread injection molding, were reasonably successful producing profits throughout the third quarter of the century. Companies such as Soennecken brought out new models during this period without feeling the need to disparage the ballpoint pen but simply treating it as another product line. In Italy the situation was similar. Fountain pens continued to sell relatively well throughout the second half of the century, again happily coexisting with their supposed archenemy.

Of course, not all people wanted to buy ballpoint pens, but the major American companies produced such poor fountain pens that the public was forced to buy other products. So throughout the second half of the century, European companies heeded perceived wisdom taught by the American companies during the first half: Hype your products, maintain quality, and sales will follow. The most obvious example of this was Montblanc, which had maintained market share and made profits even while German inflation was running rampant during the 1920s. Later on, they followed the same marketing techniques, even after they had started injection-molding throwaway components on all their products, including the most expensive. In this way, they trounced the American companies during the third quarter of the century. The American companies' owners were so scared of impacting their quarterly figures by spending money on marketing that they were quite happy to let Montblanc become the American market leader.

[2]
Wyvern lizard skin button-filler, 1930s–1940s.

[2]

CHAPTER SIX

THE FUTURE: THE REBIRTH OF THE COTTAGE INDUSTRY

At the beginning of the twenty-first century, the fountain pen business is again quite vibrant. Montblanc realized during the 1990s that they couldn't hype injection-molded products forever and that they would need a flagship product to add more substance to the hype. To this end, while the company was owned by Alfred Dunhill in the 1990s, management outside Hamburg noticed that the styling of the old products was actually quite interesting; the marketing department realized that it could give the company a great image by producing beautiful pens again. Montblanc could still produce huge quantities of injection-molded pens, but a minuscule production of flagship models would increase sales of their other lines. They have thus produced an interminable series of reasonably high-quality limited-edition pens, all of which spike in value immediately on release, until the hype of that particular limited edition is

[1]
Torelli handcrafted pen with silver cap inspired by the Parker 51.
Cap is the hand-engraved
"Empire" design. This pen was
created in 2001 after extensive
consultation with the original
plans filed in the U.S. Patent
Office for Parker's revolutionary
pen. It includes design ideas that
were never incorporated into the
production pens, such as a stepped
barrel that fits flush with the cap.
Parker was sued successfully in
1939 by the patent holder of this
feature, who prevented them from
putting it in their 51 line.
[2]
Pen from Brazil by Roberto Cafaro.
[3]
Silver Filigree Pen from England
made by Henry Simpole.
[4]
Similarly, luxurious pens are
made by hand all over the world.
This Portuguese model by Da
Costa in ivory was inspired by
worldwide collectors' love of the
Conklin design.

replaced by the next. Sheaffer suffered chronic cash shortages under a variety of diffident owners outside the pen industry, but eventually looked to the vintage pen market, where their 1960s PFM model had always sold well, and began to produce an updated version of that pen.

Even small companies like Omas and Aurora, which have always made quality pens, reasoned that emphasizing excellent production values would help sales. Omas had been successfully sponsoring a major enthusiasts' pen club and vintage pen shows to increase public awareness of their pens. During the 1990s, Omas exhibited their top lines of exceptionally beautiful faceted pens at pen shows, where they would bring their equipment to demonstrate their manufacturing processes. Those pens are still produced by hand from drilled-out rod stock, as were the best pens from the beginning of the twentieth century.

Most interesting has been the plethora of "companies"— usually individuals—starting up production of elegant hand-crafted pens to an extraordinarily high standard. Often these

[1]

[2]

[3]

[4]

pens draw their inspiration from pre-1930 designs, and occasionally, even the early filling mechanisms are faithfully replicated.

One of the best pen repairers—Torelli Pen—has started producing what are arguably the highest-quality pens available, individually designed and commissioned for each customer. These customers are often governments ordering Torelli's pens as special presentation pieces. In fact, it is said that a government department can be almost the only one who can short-circuit his waiting list that is years long—a list that virtually guarantees that the pens are among the few new pens immediately worth more as collectable products than their retail price.

So continues the corporate cycle I have described. Most of the large companies have been taken over by indifferent corporate giants whose management knows nothing of the reasons why pen companies go broke. But the slack in quality pen innovation is taken up all over the world by these individuals producing handmade offerings. In France, this is nothing new: French fountain pen production has always been something of a specialized cottage industry, centered on the companies that produce pens in small villages around the Massif Central. Today handmade pens are produced in this way by companies such as Lepine, Luthier, Recifé and Audiard. In England the flag is carried by Henry Simpole, in the United States by Bexley and Michael Fultz. This same flag is even carried in South America where pens are made in Brazil by Roberto Cafaro, and in Argentina by Sergio Kullock.

But the really curious anomaly in the fountain pen market occurs in Japan. The major fountain pen company, Pilot, has never been taken over by any corporate giant. Pilot still has a handmade high-end brand, now called Namiki again (and sometimes even Dunhill-Namiki), after the famous Dunhill-Namiki pens of the 1930s. Although it produces a very wide range of pens, it has managed to buck the boom-degrade-slump-bust-takeover cycle which has plagued

[1]

A. W. Faber Piece.

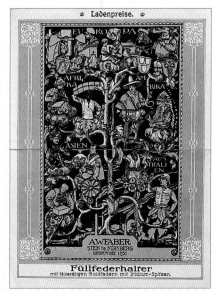

[1]

other companies.

There is a lesson to be learned from the flourishing of enthusiast-run companies. It is an eccentric lesson in that it doesn't seem to have been applied seriously to any other area of industry. Management interest in the product cannot decrease the higher up the management chain wanders. Thus management has to be able to make decisions unaffected by the short-term need to pander to accountants. If it can do this, whether the company is big or small, production and ultimately profits can flourish.

Je ne peux oublier...

Je ne peux oublier tes paroles très tendres;
Souvent je les évoque et je crois les entendre.

5396/3

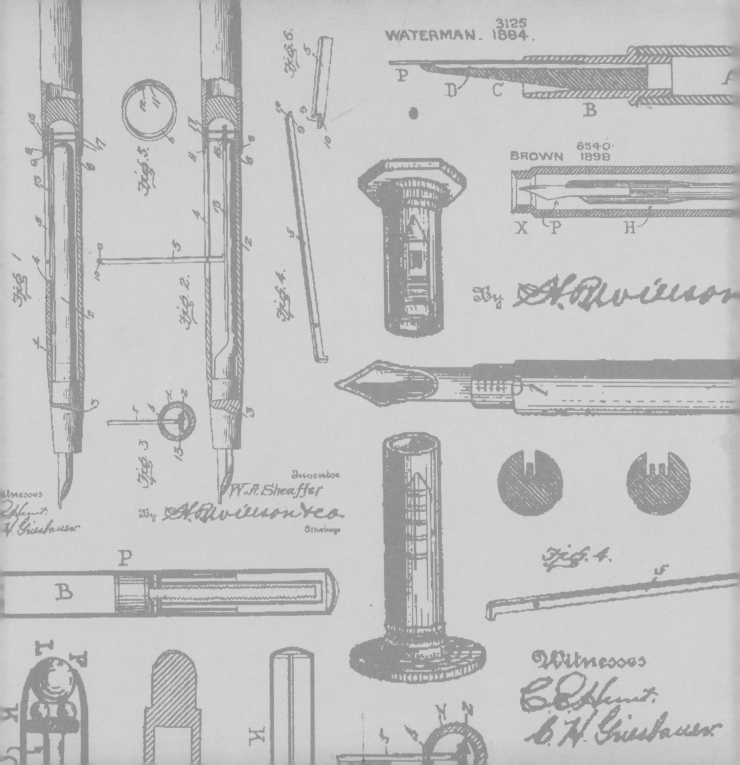

WATERMAN. 3125 1884.

BROWN 8540 1898

Fig. 1

Fig. 2

Fig. 3

Fig. 5

Fig. 6

Fig. 4

Fig. 4

Inventor
W. A. Sheaffer
By H. A. Wilson & Co.
Attorneys

Witnesses
C. E. Hunt.
C. N. Giesbauer

By H. A. Wilson

Witnesses
C. E. Hunt.
C. N. Giesbauer